Life Is Unkind

ROBERT ROGERS

To order additional copies of this book, contact:
Xlibris
844-714-8691
www.Xlibris.com
Orders@Xlibris.com

ISBN: Softcover   978-1-6698-4052-7
         EBook   978-1-6698-4051-0

Print information available on the last page

Rev. date: 08/02/2022

Contents

Good Times...1

Hard to Live Like This..2

I Do Despair..3

Dream You...4

I Drink This Way...5

I Love You..6

I miss you...7

I Remember...8

I'm Alone...9

Life is Short...10

Life's Borders...11

Love is Unkind..12

Memories...13

Monday Morning..14

My Hero...15

Never Come True..16

Sharing Feelings..17

The Feeling Lingers...18

What Is Real?...19

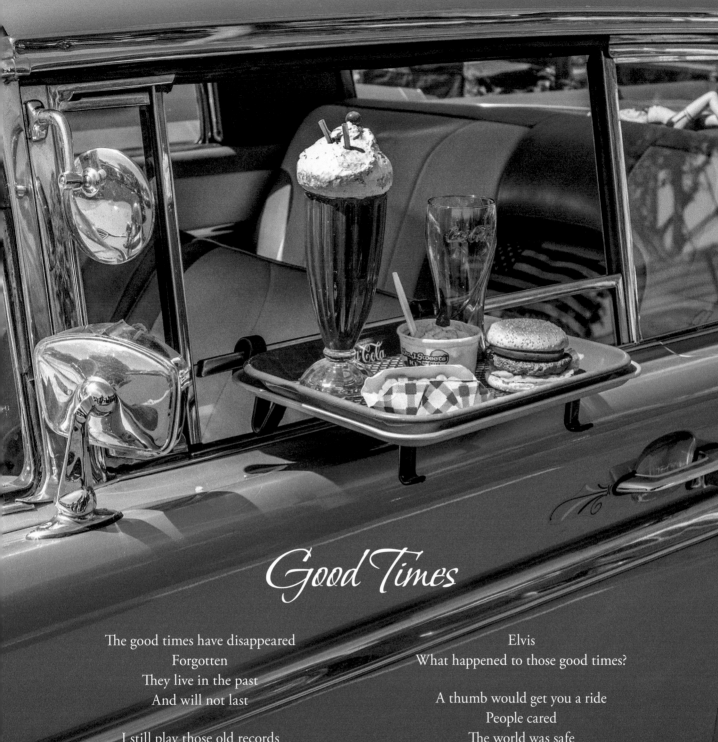

Good Times

The good times have disappeared
Forgotten
They live in the past
And will not last

I still play those old records
Remember the songs
Enjoy what I hear
Those sounds are still clear

I drove the cars that were real machines
I shifted the gears
That remains in the past
Lost

We danced to rock and role
Listened to Peter Paul and Mary

Elvis
What happened to those good times?

A thumb would get you a ride
People cared
The world was safe
No longer the case

A quarter could call someone you loved
A mobile phone has taken its place
We all have one
The phone booth disappeared

I remember the drive-in movie
The girl at my side
The kiss she would provide
What happened to those good times?

Hard to Live Like This

It's hard to live like this
I don't know why
It's just this way
I struggle from day to day

I live a single life
Others wonder why
Do they need someone else?
Why?

Can two solve my struggle?
It's hard to say
I just elect to live this way
My life may change

Can I find someone who understands?
A close relationship may not last
Will they know me?
Hard to say

Living a single life is elective
I can't say why
For me it is just this way
I do wonder why

I hope being single will change
Discover someone who cares
Change my struggle from day to day
Not elect to live this way

I Do Despair

I can't make love with you like I once could
Age has taken an eclectic pace
I do despair
I know you still care

A woman can make love all her life
A man meets strife
I want renewed preservation
Regain the loss

The pills help
But much has been lost
They aide for a time
At an unfulfilled cost

You remain the same
I distress

My wish I can't share
I do care

My world has turned upside down
I will never recover
The wanting is high
The performance cannot follow

You are the world to me
Life can be unkind
I must bide
I can't turn the tide

I love your so
My desire can't be fulfilled
The longing remains
It's life's eternal design

Dream You

I lay in bed and dream you
Will that dream ever come true?
I can only wish
Can you ever be mine?
I long to hold you
I wait to dream you again

Can dreams come true?
They are fragments of how we feel
They seldom become real
I can only wish

I want to hold you
Feel the warmth
Know you are real
Know how we both feel

Will my dream come true?
I awake and wonder
My life would change
I realize it's only a dream

Do you dream like me?
Wish your dream was real?
I wonder
We could touch

We could lay in bed together
Stop the dreams
Know what is real
Know how we feel

My dream may not come true
I silently lay there
Dream of you

I Drink This Way

I drink too much
I know shy
It's you
Because you can't be true

Don't look at me that way
I have changed
I see it in your eyes
The things you say

You made me drink this way
We once had equal love
That seems to fade
Look what you've made

A woman can be forgiving
Drink washers that away
I don't know what to say
That's why I drink this way

Liquor dulls the pain
I don't feel the same
It's you to blame
Because you can't be true

What can I do?
Put the glass away?
Ignore the things you say?
Forget what we once had?

Stumble out the door
Forgive you once more
I think not
I shall just drink this way

Live in this liquor wash
Try to forget the love we once had
Know the cost
Know what I have lost

I Love You

I'm sorry I hurt your
The reason I can't explain
The sorrow remains
My feelings were strange

Forgive me
I don' know what to say
Can you forgive me?
Tell me

Please come back to me
Look into my eyes
See them shine
Please don't decline

I'm sorry
I want to renew our love

It can be new
I do love you

Walk back to me
I want to see you
Rekindle how our love began
Hold you again

My world has changed
But my love remains
Please forgive me
Let me hold you again

Remember how our love use to be
I beg you
Return to me
I love you

I miss you

Every day I pray
You have gone to that war
I long to see you more
I hurt every day

I want you
It's a solum task
It will always last
Come back to me

When you return
We shall make love
Like we've never done before
Never keep score

Every day will be new
God, I love you

Heaven knows
You are the one I chose

I will love you forever
War shall not break us apart
Caress me
Make peaceful love with me

Walk through that front door
Hold me tight
Our love will last
Let the War remain in the past

I hope you can
Every day will be new
I do love you
Hurry back to me

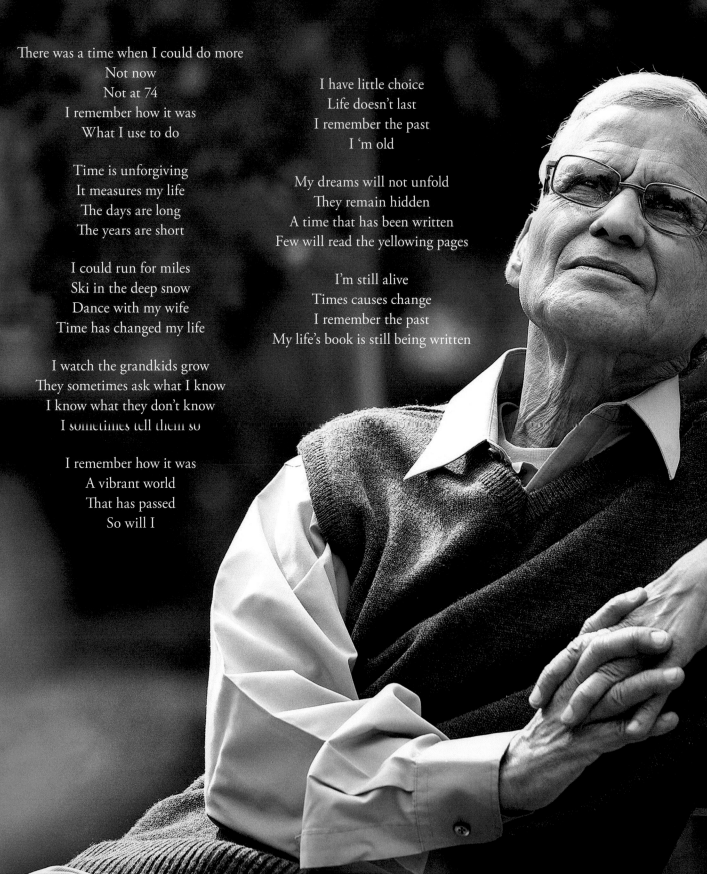

I Remember

There was a time when I could do more
Not now
Not at 74
I remember how it was
What I use to do

Time is unforgiving
It measures my life
The days are long
The years are short

I could run for miles
Ski in the deep snow
Dance with my wife
Time has changed my life

I watch the grandkids grow
They sometimes ask what I know
I know what they don't know
I sometimes tell them so

I remember how it was
A vibrant world
That has passed
So will I

I have little choice
Life doesn't last
I remember the past
I 'm old

My dreams will not unfold
They remain hidden
A time that has been written
Few will read the yellowing pages

I'm still alive
Times causes change
I remember the past
My life's book is still being written

I'm Alone

I'm here alone
You are gone
I have no place to go
I'm alone

You walked out the door
Never said a word
That closing door
is all I heard
A tragic sound

I'll call my mom
Tell her how I feel
You are searching for
something to gain
But I hope to see you again

I hurt
I may never heal
It's how I may always feel
Alone

It's raining
A reflection of how I feel
Love cannot escape
It will never wash away

My caring will
always remain
I can't hide this feeling
It will prevail
I hurt

You closed the door
Never to see you once more
I will not find another you
I may search

Life is Short

A long life was expected
I know it isn't so
The doctor says so
I have no choice

I shall do what I like
Make the best of my life
My life is short
It shall soon end

Live with grace
Hope the end is not a race
I am not afraid
Accept the event

There are others like me
They live in the moment
Accept what will be
Life reaches an ending boundary

My life is confined
It lives in a limited space
I will do what I like
Enjoy my fleeting life

Visit places where I've never been
Do some things I still can
See the Grand Canyon
Walk in an oceans beach sand

I hope I'm remembered
Lived with grace
I was not afraid
I enjoyed my life

Life's Borders

We have reached a border in our life's
Will our love remain?
It's hard to say
Our love may stray

Our lives are different patterns
We move in different ways
Love requires stitching together
Combining

We search for something new
It troubles both me and you
Time will tell
The patterns may never knit

We once enjoyed what we had
A shared love
That warmth is fading
Little is remaining

I regret how our love has changed
You feel the same
Our eyes seldom meet
We don't touch

We can't cross this border
It blocks the love we once shared
We cared
We may never again feel the same

Love is Unkind

You are unkind
You love someone else
Not me
I don't know why

Why are you leaving me?
Can you tell me?
I want to know why I'm losing you
What can it be?

When we are close
I don't see that sparkle in your eyes
Your talk is harsh
You reluctantly touch me

Why someone else?
Why not me?
Have you stopped loving me?
Tell me

Did I do something wrong?
No longer want me near
You are unkind
You will no longer be mine

Let us begin again
Don't walk away
Stay
You want someone else
That's unkind

Memories

It was the best of times
I have those memories
I remember when you said goodbye
That memory remains

We danced on that hardwood floor
It was a playground
The red dress and cowboy hat
Waylen and Cash

That love did not last
The memories fade
Live in the past
I remember what we once had

We drank a little whisky from a mason jar
Laughed and held each other
Wanted to see what we could discover
Love each other

I still see that red dress and cowboy hat
We danced
You said goodbye
I still don't know why

That red dress you no longer wear
The hat has been discarded somewhere
Our lives have changed
You simply said goodbye

I still don't know why

Monday Morning

I's Monday Morning
How bad I feel
And what do I see
A day that is killing me

I have to start all over
Struggle to stay sober
Watch the rain
I must try harder

All Mondays are the same
A happy future I just can't see
What will become of me?
A tired broken man

I hate Mondays
It's always an unpleasant beginning
A happy life I just don't see
This feeling is slowly killing me

Can I begin again?
Not a man like me
I just survive
Just stay alive

When I wake on Monday morning
I need to welcome the rain
Try harder
See what I can attain

Mend this feeling that is killing me

My Hero

I remember my dad
It was long ago
He was my hero
Greif I now know

Sad he is no more
I loved him so
He held this little girl's hand
We walked in the beach sand

I wish he was still here
Time changes things
Life is a candle
It burns bright for a short while

We walked when the sun was bright
He often held me tight

Read to me at night
Slept beside me

The stories were funny
We laughed
The people were not alone
They teased each other

Dad was a carpenter
A builder of things that last
He is my hero
I never told hm so

Life doesn't last
I remember the past
Dad and Me
A carpenter holding a young girl

15

Never Come True

We should have never met
Why have I fallen In love with you?
My wanting will never come true
It cannot last

When you held me on that dance floor
I hoped it would be for evermore
I don't know why
You will never be mine

We should have never met
My wanting I still regret
You never felt this flame
It burns deep

You held me tight
It all seemed right
The night was rose-colored
I was stary-eyed

Love with just a dance?
Puzzling wants sometimes come true
I don't know how to tell you
We have only met

The music stopped
This strange loving will never come true
I may never again dance with you
The flame can not last

Sharing Feelings

I am not going to talk to you anymore
You tell everyone how I feel
I don't want them to know
I told you so

My feelings are only for you
Our lives are private
Not to be shared
I thought you cared

How we make love Is between you and me
Others don't need to know
It's a private affair
You don't care

I'll not make love with you anymore
Not tell you how I feel
You're sharing I can no longer endure
I will not talk to you anymore

My feelings are private
Yours are not
Why tell others?
You don't care

I shall end this loving affair
Walk out the door
Not talk to you anymore
Keep my feeling secret

You will miss me
I now know you
You don't know me
Our loving has reached an end

You can tell others how you feel
I no longer care

The Feeling Lingers

You may never be mine
We met long ago
I see you in my mind
The picture is clear

The feeling lives on
When will we meet again?
Love is strange
It remains

My want lingers
It may never come true
I still want you
Will this want never end?

I want to be with you
Touch you again
Remember what touching was like
That warm feeling

Will I ever find you ?
I hope so
I just don't know
It was a long time ago

Your picture seems real
The color of your hair
Those blue eyes
I do wonder how you feel

My hope is unending.

What Is Real?

My world has changed
Stands still
I don't know what is real
Where are you?

Is this a dream?
Will I wake and find you?
Will this dream come true?
Where are you?

I search
Can you hear my heart?
It seems to be standing still
Is this real?

I have always wanted you
I now wake
Put my feet on the floor
Open the bedroom door

You are no longer here
This is not a dream
It's real
I struggle with the guilt I feel

I was the one at fault
Can't put my arms around you
Listened to what you say
I can now only dream you

Printed in the United States
by Baker & Taylor Publisher Services